THE OFFICIAL

HIBERNIA

ANN 2018

Written by David Forsyth

Designed by Ross Addy

A Grange Publication

ISBN 978-1-911287-72-8

EDEN.MILL
ST ANDREWS
SHARE OUR PASSION
EDENMILL.COM

CONTENTS

WELCOME TO THE OFFICIAL HIBERNIAN FC ANNUAL.

Season 2016/17 was always going to be challenging following the glorious high of our Scottish Cup win at the end of the previous campaign, alongside our failure to get promoted back to the Premiership.

Those twin outcomes meant that last season could have only one possible satisfactory outcome – automatic promotion through winning the Championship and avoiding the trauma of being involved in the play-offs for the fourth season running.

What a journey it was! The highs and lows of professional sport ensured an exciting rollercoaster of a ride, peppered with an exhilarating defence of the Scottish Cup. Who could forget the two Cup matches against Hearts, with a bumper sell-out crowd at Easter Road enjoying a Hibernian win and giving us a stirring rendition of "Sunshine on Leith." Or our league win against rivals Dundee United 3-0, the team blasting out of the blocks to lay down a real message of intent. In any event, at the end of the season our mission was accomplished with an eventually comfortable league win and our return to the top flight of Scottish football.

Now we face a new chapter, and one that your Club is looking forward to with optimism and excitement. We have a strong management team, we have a good and balanced squad, and we have the backing of a big and growing support.

While success at Hibernian will always be defined on the pitch, that can't happen without the efforts of a lot of other people who work tirelessly behind the scenes. And your Club continues to try to improve what we do off the pitch as well, so that we can deliver even more on the pitch for supporters to enjoy.

The Annual, as ever, has lots of terrific photographs, profiles, and fun things to do. I hope you enjoy it!

WINNING THE CHAMPIONSHIP

The Key Battle Grounds

Before the league campaign was even underway, Hibernian supporters were looking forward with some confidence following a strong performance in European competition against a top Danish side.

Hibernian had qualified for the Europa League following the Scottish Cup win in May 2016 – and had been unfortunate to draw a strong Brondby side. A narrow defeat, by 0-1 in the first leg at Easter Road, made the task even harder with a trip to Copenhagen.

However, with more match time under their belt the team travelled with quiet confidence, and put in one of our strongest European displays in years to win 1-0 away from home and take the tie to penalties, before eventually losing out. Brondby were to go on to defeat a Bundesliga side in the next round, making the Hibernian performance all the more creditable.

August

The Championship campaign kicked off on August 6, with a tough tie away at Falkirk who again promised to be major rivals. A hard fought, but deserved, 2-1 win at one of the league's most difficult venues gave a stirring start, particularly given the difficulty the team had faced in digging out wins against that dogged opposition in the previous two years.

Striker Jason Cummings netted twice to ensure the points returned to Easter Road.

League wins aganst Dunfermline (2-1), St Mirren (0-2) and Morton (4-0) followed, giving the Club a glorious August start.

September

Another tough venue was next up with an away trip to Dumbarton, who had also proved something of a bogey side in previous campaigns.

A gritty 0-1 victory continued the season's perfect start before the first defeat of the season hit with a bump when Ayr United claimed a 2-1 win against ten-man Hibs at Easter Road.

Red cards were to play a prominent part in the season, with some poor decisions being overturned on appeal. A scoreless draw away at Queen of the South was next up, with Hibernian's hopes again hampered by a red card.

October

The month of October kicked off with an eagerly anticipated match against newly-relegated Dundee United, who were expected to supply the biggest challenge to Hibernian's hopes of a title triumph. More than 15,000 fans flocked to Easter Road for the game.

A James Keatings strike put the home side in front, reflecting their dominance and reward for some exciting football. The same player had earlier struck the post from a free kick.

Midway through the second half, United levelled through a header from William Edjenguele, and despite late pressure United held out for the draw. It was the first of many feisty encounters with the Tannadice side throughout the campaign.

November

A strong performance saw Hibernian put three past Ayr United without reply away from home as the Easter Road side began November in the same style as they had ended October. Next up was the team's second encounter with Falkirk, this time at Easter Road.

As ever between the two sides, the match was tough with no quarter asked or given, and when former Hibs midfielder Tom Taiwo was red-carded for a poor challenge on John McGinn, Falkirk must have believed their chance of a win had gone.

However, a John Baird strike stunned the home support, and the Bairns looked to be heading for an unlikely victory until a late header from Paul Hanlon salvaged an important point. Hibernian were one point clear of Dundee United in the race to the title.

December

December was to prove a busy month, with five tough matches. First up was a return clash with Dundee United, at Tannadice, with the Tangerines on a long unbeaten run. It was to be a tale of two penalties.

The evenly matched contest looked to have swung Hibernian's way when Martin Boyle was upended in the box and the referee pointed to the spot. However, the little striker's effort from the penalty spot was a poor one, and was saved by Cammy Bell.

The miss was brought into sharp focus when United were awarded the penalty, and Tony Andreu made sure of his opportunity to put United a goal ahead and, despite Hibernian pressure, that was how it ended. United loudly celebrated drawing level at the top of the league with Hibernian.

A home win by 2-0 against Dumbarton followed, before 1-1 draws away at Morton and then at home to Raith Rovers. The month ended with another away fixture against big rivals Falkirk. A late and spectacular strike by on-loan midfielder Kris Commons – brought in to provide emergency cover following a number of midfield injuries – secured the points in a 2-1 win for the men in green and white.

Hibernian had nudged back to a point ahead of United, with January's opening fixture looking more and more vital.

The New Year got off to a blistering start when closest rivals Dundee United returned to Easter Road for a top of the table clash. The Dundee side had enjoyed a narrow win at Tannadice a few weeks earlier which had drawn them level with Hibs at the top of the table, their celebrations a little over the top in the view of Hibernian's players and staff who were determined to gain revenge.

Power and pace out of the blocks saw Jason Cummings strike twice in the first 26 minutes to open a comfortable lead in a match Hibernian dominated from start to finish. Loud roars greeted the appearance of "Super" John McGinn midway through the second half as the midfielder returned from lengthy injury, only to slot a solo goal ten minutes from time to ensure the three points stayed at Easter Road. Hibernian were now four points clear at the top, and had laid down an emphatic message.

Dumbarton were defeated 1-0, followed by another away win at Queen of the South, again by a single goal. Results through the month had gone Hibernian's way. A despondent United had dropped more points, and the Easter Road men ended January eight points clear.

February

February began with two 1-1 draws, at home to Ayr United and then away to Raith Rovers, with the team's performance in the latter match drawing the ire of Head Coach Neil Lennon. A home draw against Dunfermline saw the sides share four goals, but in reality Hibernian had been fortunate to take a point from the game against a spirited, energetic and skilful Pars side. Despite dropping points, Hibernian finished the season seven clear of United, who had failed to capitalise.

However, the month had been dominated by a Scottish Cup tie against the club's keenest rivals, Heart of Midlothian.

March

The shaky form continued at the start of March, as Hibs lost in Paisley to a resurgent St Mirren by 2-0. A trip to Tannadice was next up, a real crunch match, with both United and now Falkirk still chasing Hibernian, with Falkirk six points behind and United seven.

In a tough and fractious match, a Jason Cummings goal was enough to secure the points for Hibernian who moved ten points clear of United. A 2-2 draw at Easter Road against Dumbarton followed, before Falkirk returned to Easter Road as the team's nearest challengers, just six points behind (although having played a game more).

The match looked destined for a draw until Efe Ambrose headed in with around 15 minutes remaining, only for Craig Sibbald to match that effort within a minute and draw the Bairns level. A draw looked certain, until a super, curling James Keatings strike secured the three points and opened a decisive lead over Falkirk.

A scoreless home draw with Morton saw the team finish the month ten points clear at the top.

April

A 1-1 draw at Dunfermline, followed by a similar scoreline at Greenock Morton, saw Hibernian edge closer to the finish line. A home match against Queen of the South was next up, with the players knowing a win could see the title wrapped up. On the day, the team stepped up to the mark, scoring three with no reply, to clinch the Club's return to the top flight of Scottish football with goals from McGregor, Cummings, and skipper David Gray.

A 3-2 win against Raith Rovers followed, and a big away win 0-4 at Ayr against United, before the title celebrations got underway with a party at Easter Road on the final day of the season with a 1-1 draw against St Mirren, ensuring the Buddies stayed in the Championship after a long fight to avoid relegation, sparking celebrations amongst both sets of supporters and players.

DEFENCE OF THE CUP

As holders, Hibernian proudly entered the Scottish Cup in the fourth round determined to make a strong defence of the famous old trophy.

On January 21st, Hibernian ran out at Tynecastle – to meet top junior side Bonnyrigg Rose, who were making their own history in reaching that stage of the Cup having dispatched Championship side Dumbarton.

Any fears of a banana skin were short lived on the day, with Hibernian putting in a strong and thoroughly professional performance to run out 8-1 winners.

The draw for the fifth round brought a swif return to Tynecastle, this time to play the much stronger proposition of Hearts, under their new Head Coach Ian Cathro. In a bloo and thunder cup tie in front of almost 17,000, Hibernian were unlucky only to achieve a 0-0 draw at the home of their greatest rivals but that meant the replay would take place at Easter Road

The return took place ten days later, on ebruary 22nd, in front of a packed house of 2,205 at Easter Road Stadium.

n electric atmosphere saw Hibs make turbo-charged start, with goals by ummings, Holt and Shinnie giving a eserved 3-0 lead before a strike from oncalves in the 70th minute brought some nall consolation for the Jambos. The result as a clear one, however, with Hibernian ogressing to the quarter finals of the Cup the expense of Hearts.

A home draw was desired, and Hibs came out of the hat first against Ayr United – one of the few sides to win at Easter Road during the season. However, the Ayrshiremen were never really in the tie, with a comfortable 3-1 victory ensuring a return to Hampden for the holders against high-flying Premiership side Aberdeen, who were comfortable in second place and had already contested the League Cup final.

The match at Hampden on Saturday, April 22nd in front of almost 50,000 was an exciting encounter, but one which began disastrously for Hibs with Aberdeen scoring within seconds following a series of errors by the men in green. A second followed within the first 20 minutes, to open a 2-0 lead for the Reds.

However, a substitution and a change of tactics brought rewards as Hibernian began to play their way into the game, with Holt in particular bringing a physical presence that troubled the Aberdeen central defenders. It was no surprise when the big striker latched on to a cross to nod home, bringing the Hibees back into contention.

A brilliant round the corner flick from Holt to complete a one-two with McGeouch saw the midfielder slot coolly home to draw the tie level, with Hibernian now looking much the likelier team to go on and win the match.

Fate was to play a cruel role, however, with a speculative shot from Hayes taking a wicked deflection on its way to securing a hard fought 3-2 win for the Dons.

Hibernian's defence of the Cup was over, but it has been a thrilling journey all the way back to Hampden.

2016 / 17

SEASON QUIZ

1 Which midfielder was brought in from Celtic on a one-month emergency loan?

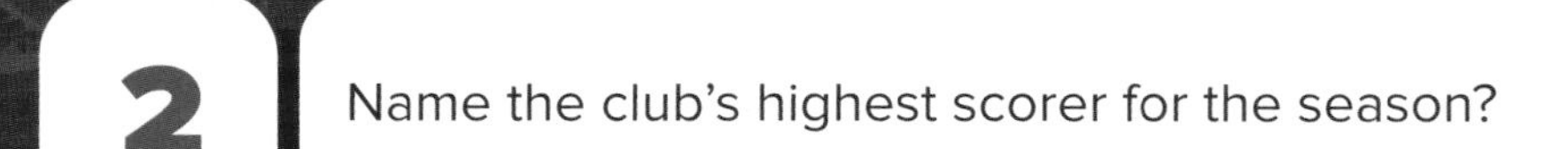

2 Name the club's highest scorer for the season?

3 What nationality is goalkeeper Ofir Marciano?

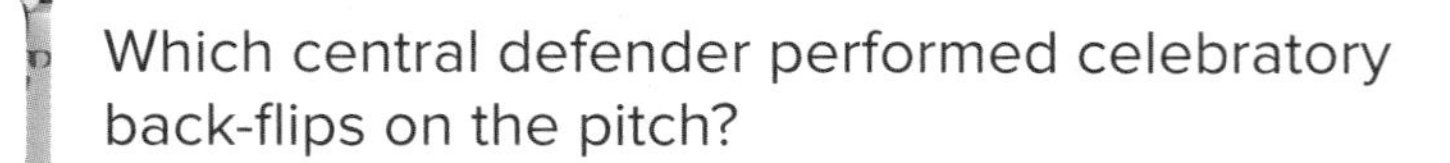

4 Which central defender performed celebratory back-flips on the pitch?

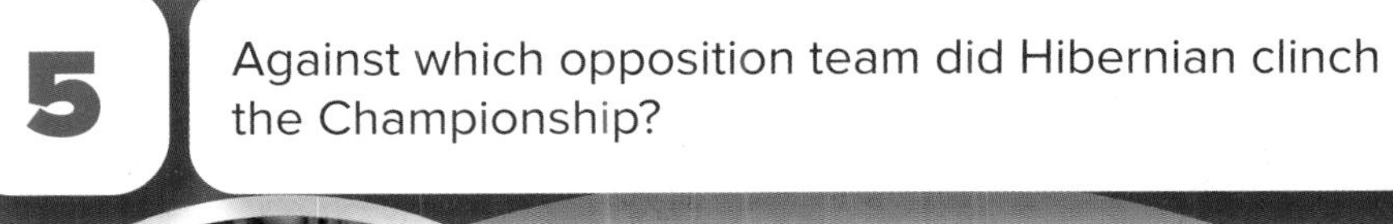

5 Against which opposition team did Hibernian clinch the Championship?

6 What was the highest goals tally scored by the Club in one match during the season?

7 Who did the Club defeat in the fifth round of the Scottish Cup?

8 Against whom did Dylan McGeouch score his solitary goal during the season?

9 Which Danish side did Hibernian play in the Europa League?

10 Who finished runners-up in the Championship?

Answers on p.58

NEW RECRUITS

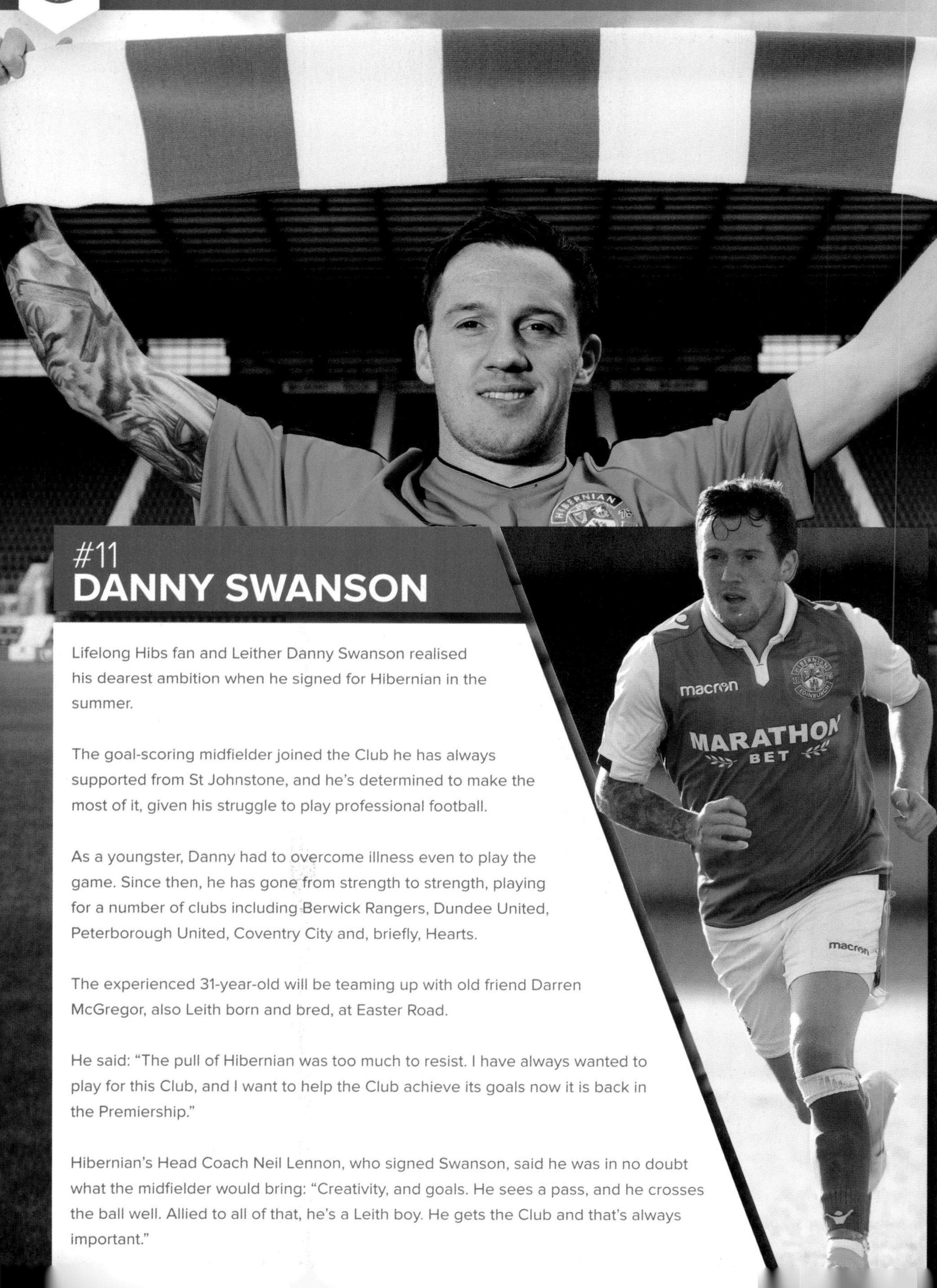

#11 DANNY SWANSON

Lifelong Hibs fan and Leither Danny Swanson realised his dearest ambition when he signed for Hibernian in the summer.

The goal-scoring midfielder joined the Club he has always supported from St Johnstone, and he's determined to make the most of it, given his struggle to play professional football.

As a youngster, Danny had to overcome illness even to play the game. Since then, he has gone from strength to strength, playing for a number of clubs including Berwick Rangers, Dundee United, Peterborough United, Coventry City and, briefly, Hearts.

The experienced 31-year-old will be teaming up with old friend Darren McGregor, also Leith born and bred, at Easter Road.

He said: "The pull of Hibernian was too much to resist. I have always wanted to play for this Club, and I want to help the Club achieve its goals now it is back in the Premiership."

Hibernian's Head Coach Neil Lennon, who signed Swanson, said he was in no doubt what the midfielder would bring: "Creativity, and goals. He sees a pass, and he crosses the ball well. Allied to all of that, he's a Leith boy. He gets the Club and that's always important."

#15
SIMON MURRAY

Striker Simon Murray was simply following a family tradition when he signed for Hibernian in the summer...

Dad Gary Murray was also a professional, who played for Montrose and Hibernian in the 1980s.

Simon joined from Dundee United, where he had enjoyed an impressive season, scoring 16 goals as United competed for the title with Hibernian for much of the season.

The pacy striker was a man in demand, with at least two other Scottish top flight clubs interested in capturing his signature and United keen to keep him.

Neil Lennon was delighted to get Murray on a two-year deal: "He's strong, he's quick and he knows how to find the back of the net. He has fantastic attributes and a real hunger to improve as well. I'm delighted he has joined."

Simon's Dad played from 1980-84, scoring 19 goals in 97 appearances.

#25
EFE AMBROSE

Nigerian international Efe Ambrose had fallen out of playing favour at Brendan Rodgers' high flying Celtic team when he joined Hibernian on loan last season.

His assured, man-of-the-match performances ensured the big defender would be back on the radar for a number of clubs, but Hibernian managed to secure him on a two-year deal.

The 6ft 3in centre-back, who can also play right-back, has more than 50 caps for Nigeria, has played for his country in the African Cup of Nations, and was named in the team of the tournament for the 2013 Cup of Nations. He also played for his country during the 2008 Olympics, and was in the squad for the 2014 World Cup.

Neil Lennon has long been a fan of this player who he managed in the Champions League for Celtic, saying: "He's a class player, and he'd walk into any team in Scotland other than Celtic at the moment. We're lucky to have him."

FONTAINE *of* KNOWLEDGE

QUESTIONS - TRUE OR FALSE?

1. Defender Darren McGregor worked in a fashionable clothes boutique just ten years ago.
2. Sir David Gray was knighted for services to Hibernian.
3. Neil Lennon's early sporting prowess was on the Gaelic football field.
4. Ofir "Rocky" Marciano has boxed professionally.
5. Lewis Stevenson is the Club's longest-serving player.
6. Liam Fontaine is also a singer/songwriter.
7. Marvin Bartley helped serve Christmas meals to homeless people.
8. Tam McCourt is a registered player.
9. Efe Ambrose enjoyed two separate league title winning celebrations last season.
10. New recruit Danny Swanson is a life-long Hibee.

Answers on p.58

BIG MARV

Q. Who is the best practical joker at Hibs?
A. The best practical joker is either John McGinn, he's got good banter and is always messing around, or Martin Boyle because he likes to annoy me a lot of the time.

Q. How did you celebrate winning promotion?
A. All of the squad went out as a team and had a night out. I also FaceTimed my partner and she was delighted with what happened.

Q. Toughest opponent you've played against?
A. I played against Adel Taarabt, he played for QPR and Tottenham, he was a special player. It's either him or Fernando Forestieri who is now at Sheffield Wednesday. Both are very, very good players.

Q. Favourite Hibs song?
A. I like the "Hibs, Hibs" song that goes to the tune of "Runaround Sue", but the best player chant is Darren McGregor's, that's quite catchy.

Q. Best player you've played with?
A. It's hard to choose just one all-round player, but in each position it would be; defender Kieran Trippier who is now at Spurs and recently got his England call-up, midfielder Darren Anderton, it was the end of his career, but he was still head and shoulders above the level he was playing at, and the best striker is Charlie Austin because he's a natural goalscorer at any level and if I don't pick him and he sees this I'll be in trouble!

Q. If you ruled the world - first thing you'd change?
A. I would change the fact that there is so much suffering in the world. Between terror attacks, people living in the street and disasters like Grenfell Tower there is a lot of pain, that's something I'd change.

Q. Whose shirt would you most like to have?
A. For a current player it would be Cristiano Ronaldo, but for a player from the past it would have to be Thierry Henry.

#21
ROSS LAIDLAW

Hibernian goalkeeper Ross Laidlaw stands an imposing 6ft 4in tall. He joined the Club in July 2016, and made his debut in a European tie against Danish crack side Brondby in Copenhagen, playing his part as Hibernian overturned a 0-1 deficit from the home tie and forced the match to extra time and penalties.

He made 18 appearances for the Club during their Championship-winning season, ably deputising for on-loan Israeli international Ofir Marciano during his injury.

Ross started his career at Raith Rovers, before signing for Hibernian on a one-year deal. He earned the two-year deal he signed in the summer of 2017.

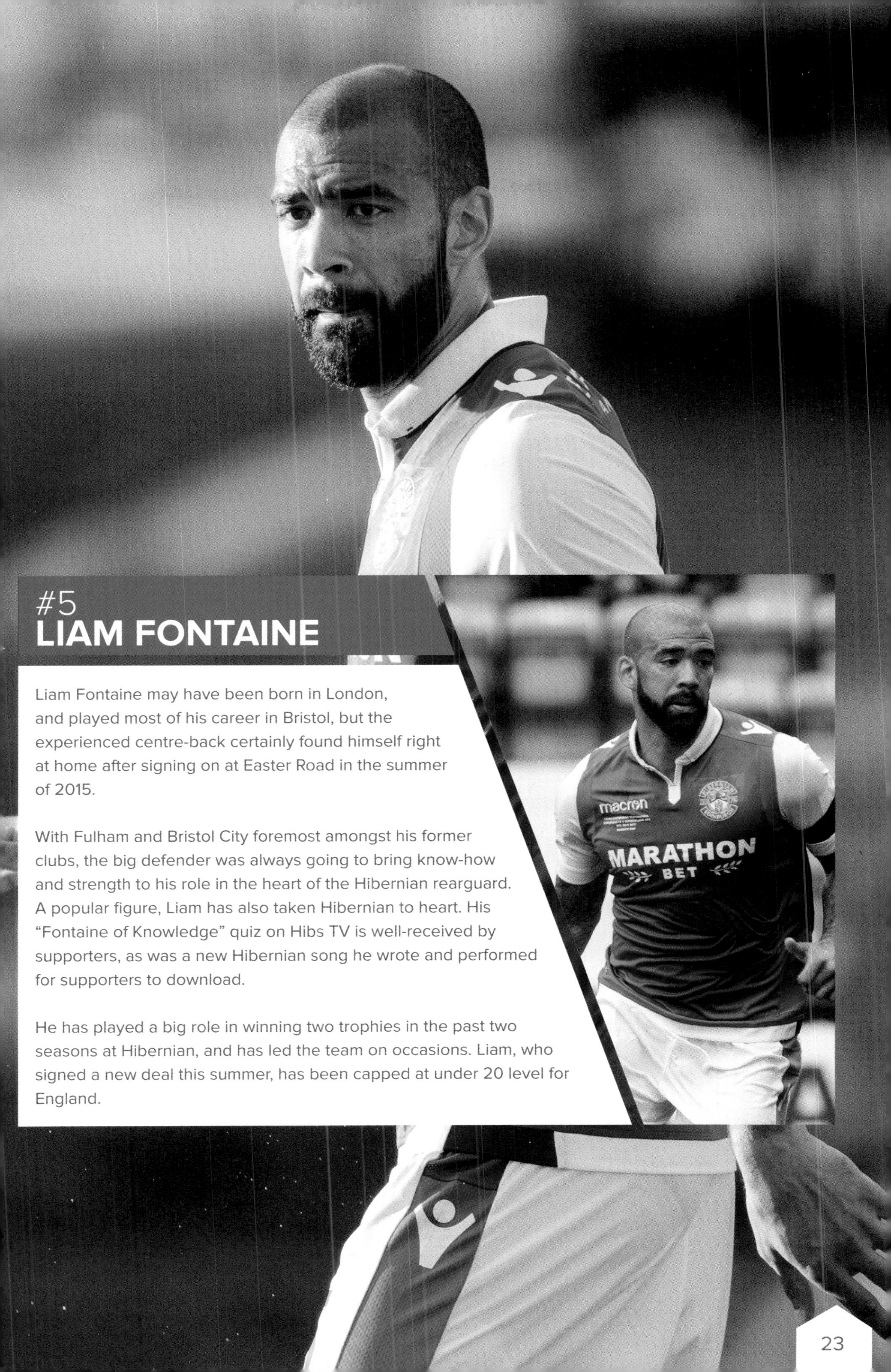

#5
LIAM FONTAINE

Liam Fontaine may have been born in London, and played most of his career in Bristol, but the experienced centre-back certainly found himself right at home after signing on at Easter Road in the summer of 2015.

With Fulham and Bristol City foremost amongst his former clubs, the big defender was always going to bring know-how and strength to his role in the heart of the Hibernian rearguard. A popular figure, Liam has also taken Hibernian to heart. His "Fontaine of Knowledge" quiz on Hibs TV is well-received by supporters, as was a new Hibernian song he wrote and performed for supporters to download.

He has played a big role in winning two trophies in the past two seasons at Hibernian, and has led the team on occasions. Liam, who signed a new deal this summer, has been capped at under 20 level for England.

#16
LEWIS STEVENSON

Left-back Lewis Stevenson enjoyed a testimonial year in 2017 – a ten-year, one-club man in an age where such a thing is increasingly rare.

A testimonial dinner held in his honour attracted many hundreds of supporters along, and included a live performance by Hibs-daft stars, The Proclaimers, as a measure of the esteem in which the popular defender is held.

Lewis holds a unique place in Hibernian folklore – the only player to have won both League Cup and Scottish Cup winners medals. He could hit close to 400 appearances for the Club this season.

Described by every manager he has played under as a model professional, the quiet and unassuming player is happier out of the spotlight but has enjoyed the two immediately past trophy winning seasons, describing them as his happiest time at the Club.

#24
DARREN MCGREGOR

A Leither, a life-long Hibernian fan and quite simply, one of our own. Darren McGregor may have started a little later than most professional footballers, but he has certainly made up for lost time in his career.

Since joining the Club from Rangers on a two-year contract, extended by two more years this summer, the big centre-half has become a firm fixture in the first team following a string of top performances that saw many pundits link him with the national squad.

During the 2016/17 season, he won the Club's Player of the Year award, and he also captained the side in the absence of David Gray. His two goals against Queen of the South helped to secure the Ladbrokes Championship title and the Club's return to the Premiership.

Darren is a major supporter of the Club's work in the community. He is the GameChanger ambassador, helping to promote healthy living in the local community - with Darren even helping out at last year's Christmas Day event at Easter Road Stadium.

PLAYER PROFILES

#2
DAVID GRAY

Sir David Gray was the first signing made by Alan Stubbs in July 2015 and an astute piece of business it has proven to be.

The Club's skipper, David was also "knighted" by Hibernian's supporters for his late, match-winning goal on May 21st 2016 – that Day – as Hibernian finally lifted the Scottish Cup.

The right-back signed a new two-year deal in the summer, tying him to the Club till 2019.

Mr Consistency, it was entirely appropriate that it was the captain who scored to round off the 3-0 win that saw the Club secure its return to the top flight of Scottish football.

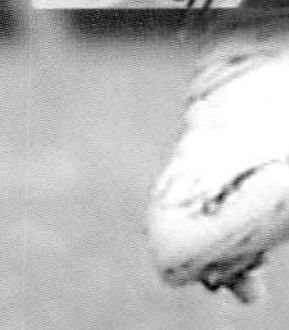

#4
PAUL HANLON

Defender Paul Hanlon passed the 300 appearances mark for the Club last season, before injury brought his campaign to a premature end.

The centre-back, who can also play full-back, played a prominent role during the season – little surprise given his consistency of selection under a number of managers since making his debut back in 2009 against Inverness Caledonian Thistle.

A product of the Club's Academy, Paul played a big part in the winning Scottish Cup run, most memorably scoring the late equaliser against Hearts at Tynecastle which forced the replay at Easter Road, and the rest, as they say, is history...

#6
MARVIN BARTLEY

Marvin Bartley signed on a two-year deal in the summer of 2015, but is another who is happy to stay at Easter Road and extended his stay this summer for another two years.

The midfield enforcer had an outstanding campaign, and his strength, pace and positional qualities will be important for the team on the return to top flight action.

Happily, the experienced professional – who has also enjoyed spells in England with Bournemouth, Burnley and Leyton Orient – has enjoyed two successful seasons, winning the Scottish Cup and the Ladbrokes Championship in successive years.

Marvin has become a fans' favourite, and as well as his on-field abilities he has also demonstrated a willingness to get involved in good causes, which has endeared him to supporters.

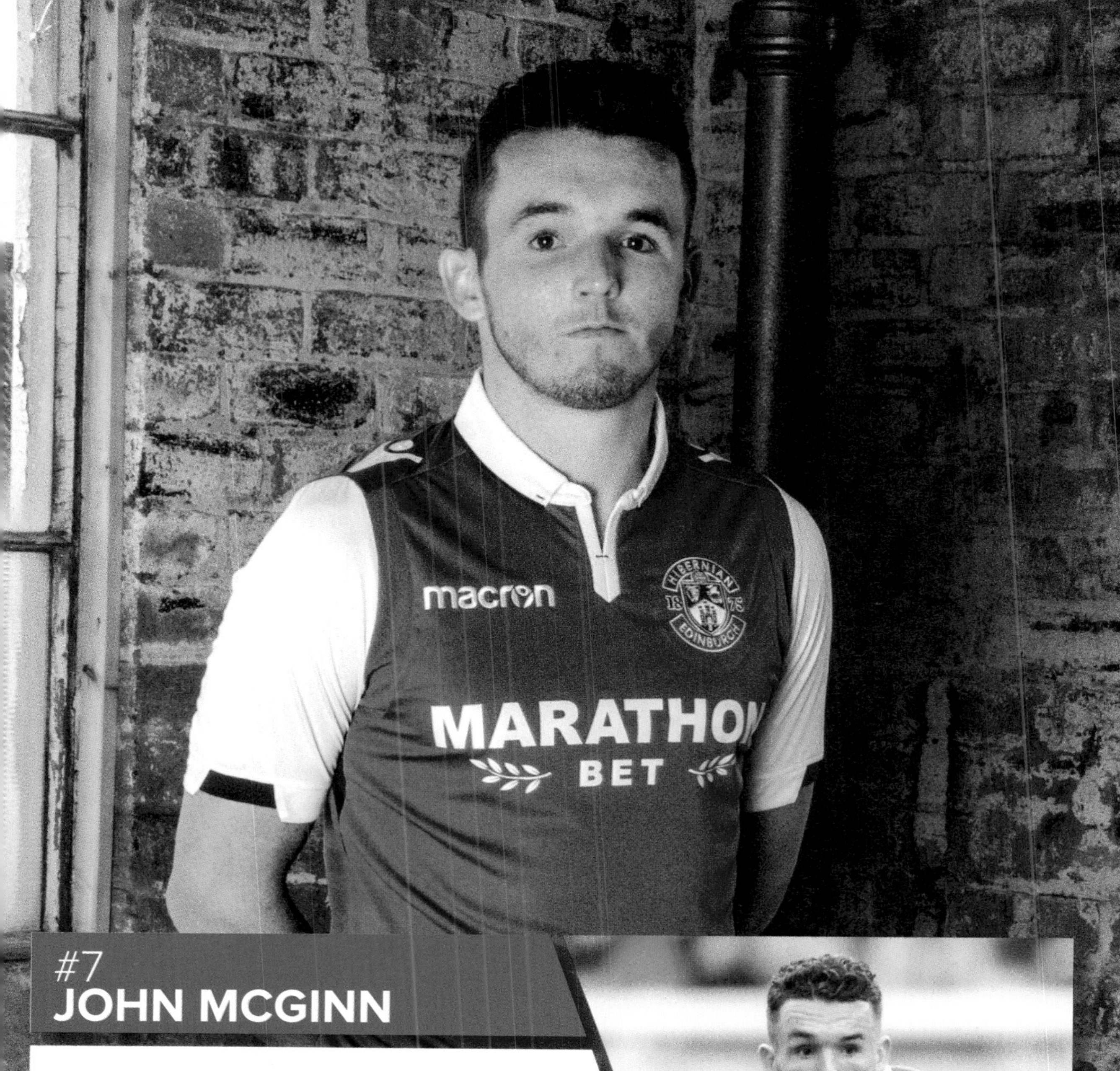

#7
JOHN MCGINN

Scotland international midfielder "Super" John McGinn has been a big factor in the resurgence of Hibernian.

The former St Mirren player joined the Club in July 2015 on a four-year contract, for an undisclosed fee. Since then, he has been priceless with his contribution to the Scottish Cup win and securing the Ladbrokes Championship.

Strong, dynamic, and with a keen eye for a pass, the all-action midfielder has caught the eye with a string of man-of-the-match performances which propelled him to international recognition despite being, at that time, in the Championship.

Often the driving force of the team, he also chipped in with five goals last season – including one stunning 40 yard strike at Somerset Park against Ayr United.

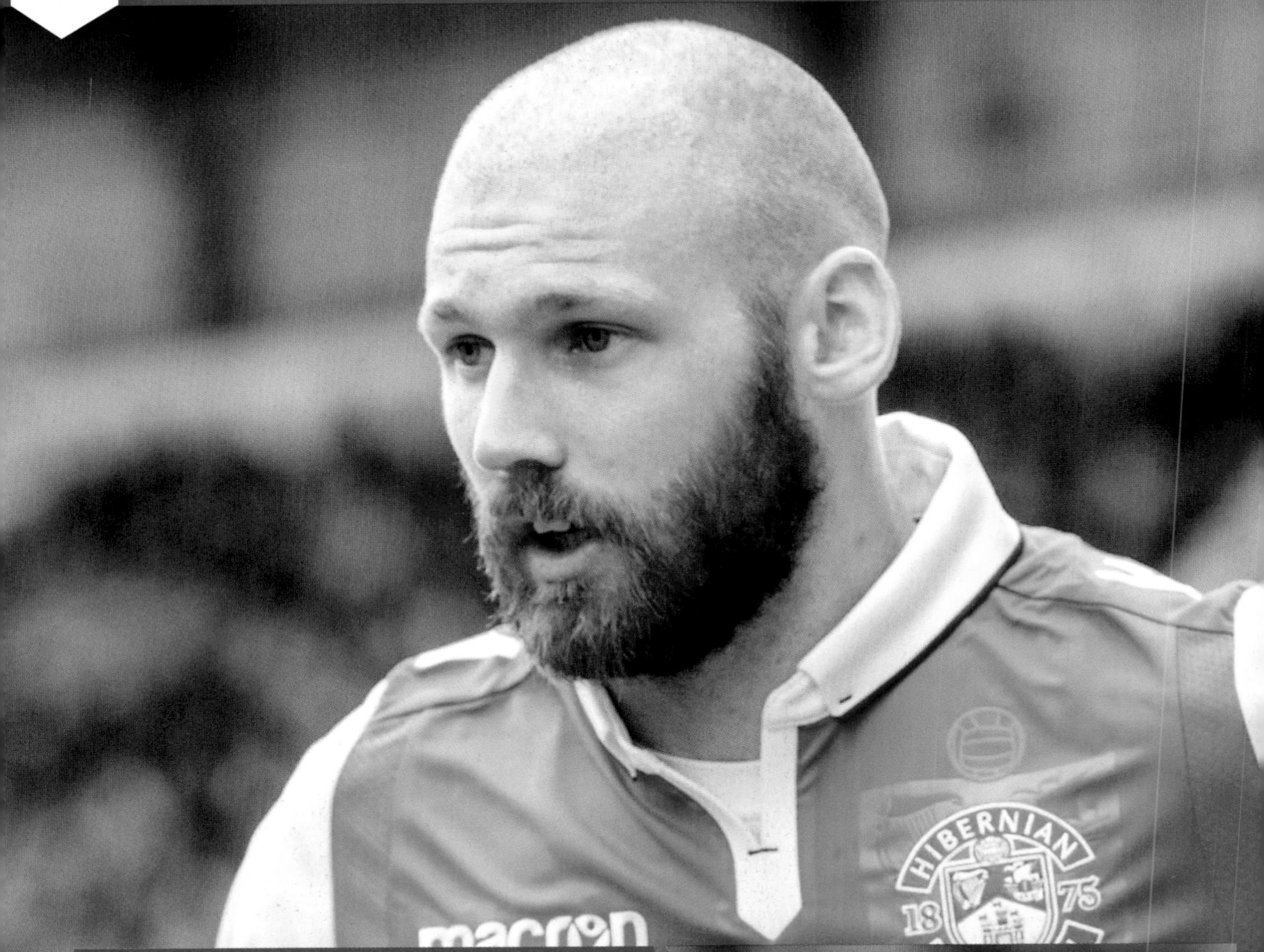

#17
MARTIN BOYLE

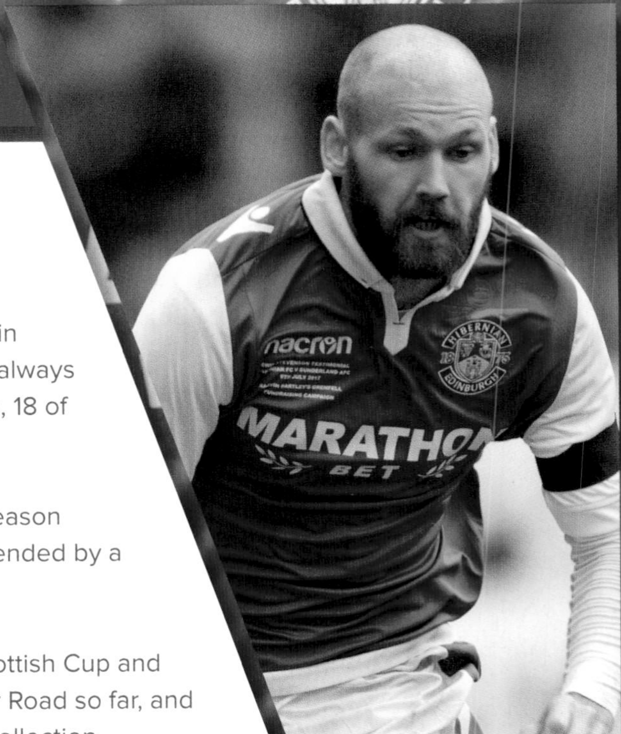

Attacker Martin Boyle has firmly established himself with the Hibernian support for his non-stop, committed displays.

"Squirrel" can play wide or through the middle, and in either position supporters know the little striker will always give 100 per cent – as well as chipping in with goals, 18 of them so far in his Hibernian career.

Martin joined on loan from Dundee in the 2014/15 season before signing a two-year deal, which has been extended by a further two years this summer.

He has been a winner during his two years, with Scottish Cup and Championship medals to show for his time at Easter Road so far, and players and fans will be hoping he can add to that collection.

#10 DYLAN MCGEOUCH

Attacking midfielder Dylan McGeouch joined Hibernian from Celtic in the summer of 2015 for an undisclosed fee – following a successful season-long loan spell the season before.

Signed up on a three-year deal, Dylan will be hoping that this season sees him avoid the injuries that have negatively impacted his time at Hibernian so far.

Despite his absences, Dylan has been a big player for the Club when he has been fit, through his high energy style and his intelligent use of the ball and reading of the game.

Formerly on the books of Rangers as well as Celtic, Dylan has also had a spell in England on loan to Coventry City.

#29 RYAN PORTEOUS

This promises to be a breakthrough season for 18-year-old central defender Ryan Porteous.

The local boy, who grew up a Hibs fan, made his competitive debut in the Betfred League Cup home win over Montrose, giving an assured display. He forced his way into first-team contention following strong performances in pre-season friendlies, and following a positive loan spell spent with Edinburgh City the previous season.

As well as showing defensive strength and aggression, the teenager showed he is willing to go in where it hurts at the other end of the pitch when he netted twice in the League Cup against Arbroath.

PLAYER PROFILES

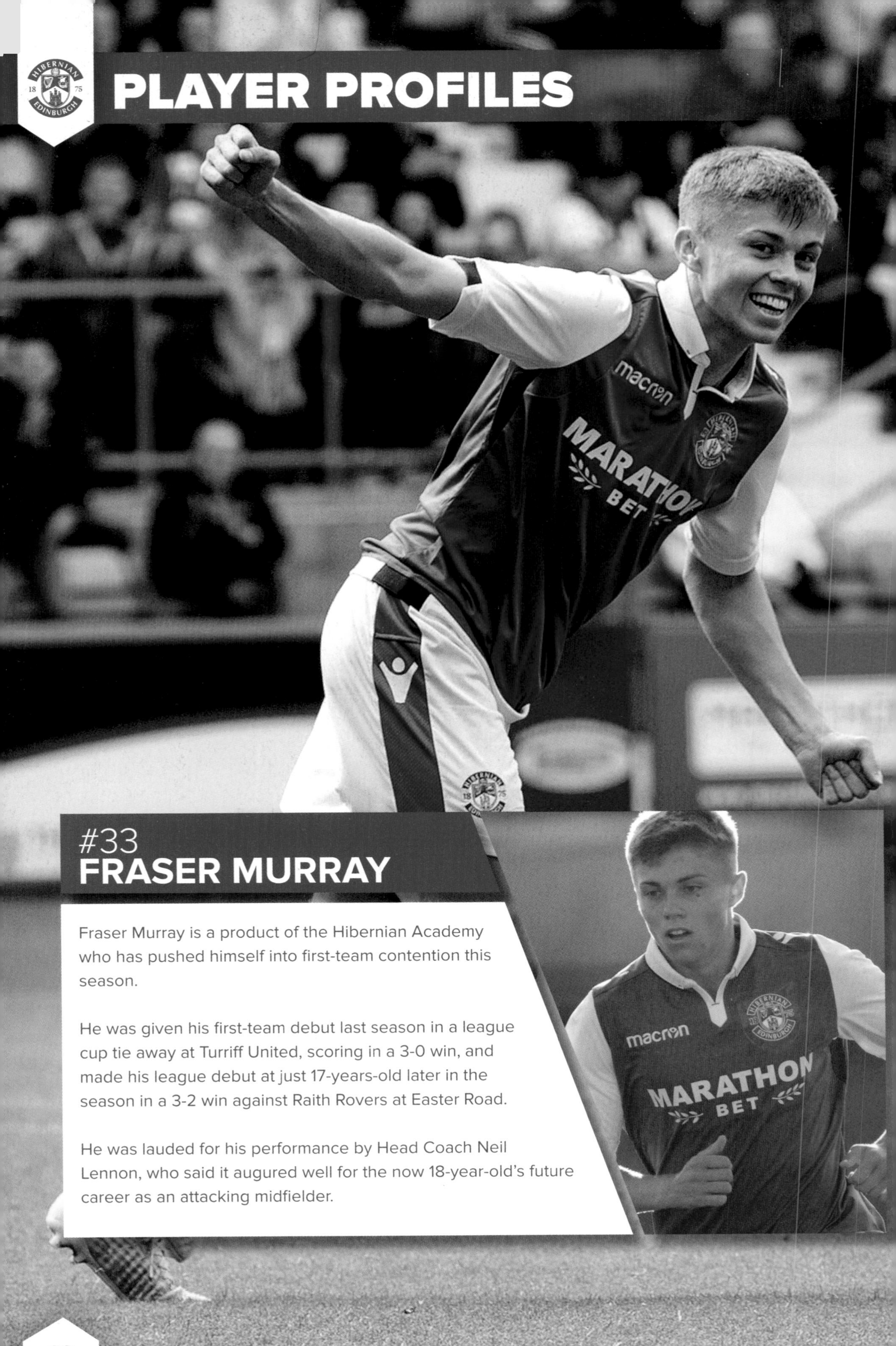

#33 FRASER MURRAY

Fraser Murray is a product of the Hibernian Academy who has pushed himself into first-team contention this season.

He was given his first-team debut last season in a league cup tie away at Turriff United, scoring in a 3-0 win, and made his league debut at just 17-years-old later in the season in a 3-2 win against Raith Rovers at Easter Road.

He was lauded for his performance by Head Coach Neil Lennon, who said it augured well for the now 18-year-old's future career as an attacking midfielder.

#26
SCOTT MARTIN

This season may be the breakthrough year for Academy graduate Scott Martin.

A Scotland under 19 international, the midfielder has been on the fringes of the first team squad for the past two seasons, making a number of appearances.

His progression through the ranks of the Development Squad has led to his inclusion in the first team squad this season.

He made his senior debut against Falkirk in December 2014, and scored his first goal in the Scottish League Cup first round tie against Montrose at Easter Road in a 3-0 win.

#32
OLI SHAW

Hopes are high for teenage striker Oli Shaw within the ranks of Hibernian coaching staff and supporters.

The 19-year-old Academy graduate has been added to the first team squad following strong seasons at development level and is a Scotland under 19 international.

The rangy six-footer played on loan for Stenhousemuir in League One last season, and despite the side having a difficult season ending in relegation, Oli scored six goals in 23 appearances.

His father, Greg, is a former professional player for a number of Scottish clubs including Dunfermline and Falkirk.

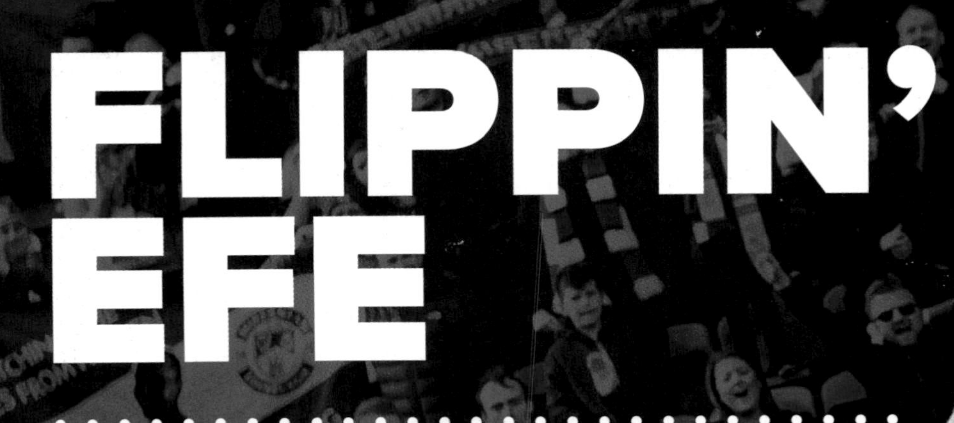

FLIPPIN' EFE

His goal – and Championship title-winning – celebrations lit up Easter Road, and Hibernian fans will be looking forward to Efe Ambrose continuing to be Flippin' Efe.

The big Nigerian defender's trademark celebration is an acrobatic series of back-flips. And while it might give coaching and medical staff the shakes as the player rotates like an Olympic gymnast, it certainly delights supporters.

As the players celebrated the winning of the Championship and the presentation of the trophy at Easter Road last season, fans urged the centre-half to perform – and he duly obliged.

He also performed a dramatic back-flip from on top of sponsor boards during Celtic's title celebrations, and once memorably performed for a 5-year-old girl in the car park at Parkhead!

While we may prefer to see him tumbling head over heels in celebration on the pitch, you can be sure things won't be dull when Efe is around to celebrate.

HiBS KiDS

Every home matchday sees some lucky youngsters fulfil a dream by leading the team out in front of thousands of Hibernian supporters at Easter Road.

The chance to be a matchday mascot is one of the many benefits membership of Hibs Kids delivers for just £15. Available for 0-11 year olds, the following is included in the membership:

- A ticket to four Hibs Kids matches a season.
- Hibs Kids membership card which can be used to gain access to Easter Road on matchdays*.
- A birthday card delivered to your registered address.
- Hibernian FC wallchart.
- Hibernian FC sticker.
- The opportunity to be a mascot at every Hibernian home league match this season (2 per match, 11 for Hibs Kids matches)

Season ticket holders are automatically Hibs Kids members, and get a wallchart and sticker, birthday card and the opportunity to be a mascot.

To join Hibs Kids simply purchase a membership online through the Hibernian eTicketing site or visit the Hibernian Ticket Office.

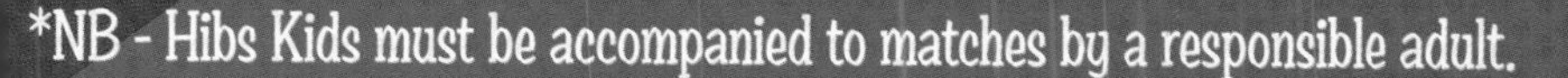
*NB - Hibs Kids must be accompanied to matches by a responsible adult.

JOHN McGINN

Hibernian fans are delighted that their team has "Super John McGinn" to drive the team

The 23-year-old came to the Club in the summer of 2015, and since then has gone on to establish himself as a full Scotland international.

Already the dynamic midfielder has collected two major trophies – the League Cup with previous club St Mirren in 2013 as the Saints defeated Hearts, and the Scottish Cup in 2016 as Hibernian defeated Rangers by the same score line – 3-2.

He was also key to the winning of last season's Championship under Neil Lennon, being named as PFA Scotland Championship Player of the Year in the process.

His all-action style coupled with his range of passing and shooting power look set to ensure there are more honours to come – and Hibernian fans will be hoping that they are in the famous green and white of Hibernian so that they can continue to sing "We've got McGinn, Super John McGinn."

But John isn't just a vital player on the pitch, he is also a big part of the dressing room camaraderie off the pitch. Here he gives a unique insight into the spirit that has seen Hibernian return to the top flight of Scottish football:

Who has been your daftest team-mate, and why?

I'll go with a surprising one and say Martin Boyle, for the fact that he is the silliest guy I've come across. Most people would say Jason, but he's actually smarter than what most people think, so it has to be Martin Boyle.

Name the best singer in the dressing-room?

David Gray. Liam Fontaine will not be happy, but after hearing his performance at his wedding, it's David.

Which team-mate has the best dress-sense – and who has the worst?

Best dress sense last year was Andrew Shinnie, he was like a model, but this year I would say Liam Fontaine. He knows how to dress well, but it helps when you have a neatly trimmed up beard! The worst dressed is either Ross Laidlaw or Martin Boyle. I'm up there as well...

How did you feel when Hibs fans first sang the "Super John McGinn" song?

It was a bit strange, I'd never heard that many people singing my name, it was a great feeling to hear it. It gives me an extra wee edge every time I play – it's always nice to hear.

Most memorable moment in football?

Winning the Scottish Cup in the same year as winning my first Scotland cap. Both were unbelievable experiences for me and it's hard to choose between the two. If I had to choose it would be winning the Scottish Cup with Hibs.

Favourite player in world football?

Lewis Stevenson!

Which country would you most like to play in, and why?

It would be Germany. I like the way they play their football. I went to a Hertha Berlin match when I had some time off a couple of years ago and I got a bratwurst outside. I like the thought of getting a win under the belt and going for a nice big hotdog outside.

HIBERNIAN HISTORICAL TRUST

Hibernian Stadium Tours are increasingly popular with Hibernian supporters keen to learn more about their Club's notable history.

The tours give fans a chance to walk through the dressing rooms, the tunnel, see rare Hibernian shirts and artefacts on display in the Board Room and take in each stand at our home, all with an expert guide.

Tours are priced at £10 per adult, £7.50 per concession and £5 per child, with discounts for large bookings. Group Bookings are also available on different dates and times to suit you.

Gift vouchers for the Stadium Tour can be purchased, a perfect birthday or Christmas present for the Hibernian supporter in your life.

For more information on booking tours or purchasing gift vouchers, contact 0131 656 7079, or visit the website on www.hibernianfc.co.uk.

Many of the achievements and work to date has been made possible through various fundraising activities, including donations from individuals, businesses, supporters' organisations and funding received from grant applications.

You can help either through donating memorabilia, money, or in other ways. Learn more at www.hibshistoricaltrust.org.uk.

CONTALMAISON AND A TRUE HIBERNIAN HERO

Club Historian Tom Wright led a club delegation to the French town of Contalmaison in the summer – to lay a wreath at a special memorial.

McCrae's Battalion Great War Memorial commemorates the dead of the 16 Royal Scots Volunteer Battalion, formed by Sir George McCrae, which became known as McCrae's Battalion or The Sporting Battalion because of the footballers from Clubs in the south east of Scotland who volunteered to serve in it during the First World War.

Players from Hibernian, city rivals Hearts, Raith Rovers, Dunfermline and Falkirk along with other sports clubs joined up. Contalmaison was a strategic target at the heart of the Somme sector action, which cost tens of thousands of lives in July 2016.

The memorial and its cairn were designed by historian Jack Alexander, and were unveiled in 2004. As such it is the last of the Great War Memorials to be built, and a wreath laying ceremony each year is attended by French and British dignitaries, as well as club representatives.

Tom said: "During the visit trips were made to several of the Commonwealth War cemeteries that surround the area including the one at the village of Roeux. It was at the battle for Roeux and the nearby Greenland Hill in 1918 that the Hibs player Alexander 'Sandy' Grosert would win the Military Cross for his actions in the face of the enemy.

"His citation reads; 'Awarded the Military Cross for conspicuous gallantry in charge of a platoon during the operation near Roeux on 27th August 1918. When the troops on his left flank and the enemy made a determined bombing attack on his position he continued to go over the open ground under fire from one post to another directing and encouraging the men. He held on until only four of the men were left and he was almost surrounded.'"

PAUL HANLON

2018 will be a big year for Paul Hanlon – marking ten years since he made his debut for Hibernian FC.

FACT FILE

- Born January 20 1990.
- Paul tops 6ft in height.
- He spent most of the 08-09 season on loan to St Johnstone, where he played full-back.
- Paul has played for Scotland at under 19 and under 21 level, skippering at both levels.
- He captained the first team at just 22-years-old.
- He scored his first goal for the Club against Falkirk.
- He has been red-carded once in his senior career.

A Hibs fan, Paul made his first senior appearance for the Club in January 2008 when he turned out against Inverness Caledonian Thistle in the Scottish Cup because of injuries to David Murphy and long-term team-mate Lewis Stevenson.

A product of Hutchison Vale and the Hibernian Academy, Paul has since gone on to make more than 300 appearances in the famous green and white, scoring 8 goals along the way.

A defender, Paul has played most of his football at centre-half, but he can also play at full-back. He signed a new three-year deal with the club in the summer of 2016 following the famous Scottish Cup win.

"This is the Club I have always supported and I love playing for. If I finish my career here, I'll be so proud."

The former Tynecastle High pupil has been a mainstay of the Hibernian defence since making his debut all those years ago, and in that time he has known a lot of highs and lows.

The lowest points for him were back to back defeats in the Scottish Cup Finals against Hearts and Celtic and relegation from the Scottish Premier League. "Hard to separate them" he says "although the defeat to Hearts felt hardest. There have been some hard times."

No doubting the high point though. Winning the Scottish Cup in 2016 elevated Paul and his team-mates to legendary status amongst the Hibernian support after bringing the 114-year wait to a dramatic end.

But the team might never have made it to the Hampden final had Paul not scored a goal that helped greatly along the way, and also helped erase one of Paul's low points.

A last-gasp equaliser from the big defender at Tynecastle capped a brilliant comeback from 0-2 down against the Jam Tarts, forcing a replay at Easter Road which Hibernian won 1-0 to progress to the quarter finals, where holders Inverness Caledonian Thistle were dispatched. Dundee United were seen off after penalties in a tense semi, before the big day against favourites Rangers in the May sunshine.

May 21, 2016 will live long in the memory, when another tremendous late fightback saw Hibernian come back from 2-1 down to clinch the old trophy with a 3-2 win.

Paul reflects: "It was the best day. As a Hibs fan you know all about the Cup run, and you are desperately hoping to win it. So when we finally did, it was just surreal. It was brilliant, and it was great to give that to the fans after all they had been through."

Paul has been part of a mean Hibernian defence in recent seasons, partnering with Darren McGregor or Liam Fontaine. His fine form saw many pundits advocating both himself and Darren McGregor for Scotland call-ups. To the media, Darren played down such talk, modestly describing himself as "an old cart-horse" before adding his name to those suggesting his team-mate had earned a chance at international level.

Perhaps, with the Club's return to the top flight, this could be the year that Paul adds full honours to his age-group caps.

SPOT THE BALL

Can you guess which is the real ball?

Answer on p.58

NEW RECRUITS

#28
ANTHONY STOKES

Star striker Anthony Stokes, whose Cup Final double helped fire the Club to the Scottish Cup in May 2016, rejoined Hibernian in the summer.

Stokes, 29, is enjoying his third spell at the club, following his times here in 2009 and 2016.

Anthony said: “The club has a big place in my heart and it’s where I’ve played some of my best football. The scenes of celebration following the cup win will live long in my memory, and the only disappointment from my last spell was that we didn’t get promotion.

“The boys did brilliantly last season and now I’ll be looking to help us push on back in the Premiership.”

#20
BRANDON BARKER

Brandon Barker joined Hibernian on a one year loan deal in August.

The Manchester City player – who has featured in a cup match for the English giants – was the final transfer window business.

The 20-year-old, who has represented England at age group levels up to under 20, brings more pace and trickery to the team, and hopes to emulate the success of Manchester team-mate Patrick Roberts, who has enjoyed loan spells at Celtic.

Brandon said: “I know Pat well from City and the national teams, and he has done fantastically well, but I just thought that this was the best move for me. I am delighted to be here.”

GARY MURRAY

SIMON MURRAY

LIKE FATHER LIKE SON

When Hibernian signed striker Simon Murray from Dundee United in the summer the Club was getting more than a striker who'd bagged 18 goals during the season...

The pacey hitman was bringing some family history with him when he joined the squad at Easter Road – following in the footsteps of his dad, Gary.

LIKE FATHER LIKE SON

Excited as he was to be in the stunning new surroundings of the Hibernian Training Centre, and at the prospect of playing at Easter Road Stadium, he couldn't help but feel at home pretty quickly.

Simon said: "I was brought up listening to tales of Dad's time in football, and in particular his time at Hibs. He has a real soft spot for the Club, playing here in the 1980s for a few years before injury finished his career early.

"He got a bit emotional when he knew I was signing for Hibs"

"He came down with me when I signed. He was here a good few years ago so they never had a facility like this. I think they were just at a public park. I remember him mentioning they were running up dunes.

"He loved it when he came through. He loved the look of the place, the facilities are just amazing and he knows it can only help me improve."

Murray Senior was nicknamed "Charger" for his bustling, never-say-die style of play – and workrate plays a big part in the style of Simon.

He said: "I suppose I do play a bit the same way, in that I am happy to chase lost causes. Part of that is my attitude, I guess. I didn't come through the Academy route, I played part-time and worked as a plumber until Dundee United gave me my chance to go full-time.

"Obviously Dundee United, where I have come from, have a good history themselves, they are a big Scottish Club. But coming through to Edinburgh, seeing the fans, seeing those season ticket figures, it's amazing the size of this club. It's exciting."

Gary Murray - back row, second from left

Back in 1980, dad Gary was signed for the Club by then manager Bertie Auld, from Montrose. A knee injury suffered in a reserve game was to cut short his career, but in his spell at Hibernian he managed to notch 18 goals in 80 appearances, including two in one match against Celtic.

No-one was more pleased with the move for Simon than Gary. "When he told me it came out of the blue, but I was chuffed to bits. It is fantastic to see him at Hibs, and I was overjoyed when he told me."

He also believes his son is set to surpass his days at Easter Road: "Simon is a better player than I was, already, and he will improve still further. His two seasons at Dundee United have been his first two seasons of full-time football, and he has come on leaps and bounds. He now has the chance to go on and make a real name for himself in the top flight with a big Club like Hibs.

"I couldn't be prouder."

WHAT'S IN A NAME?

Nicknames have probably been around since names were first created – but the word nickname dates back centuries to the 1400s, and comes from eke-name. The old word, eke, means to add, to increase, or to lengthen.

Nicknames have always been part and parcel of football – both those bestowed on players by team-mates or opponents and those who have earned the soubriquet from fans on the terraces.

Some have been highly descriptive of a style of play – "Jinky" to describe the mazy dribbling of legendary Celtic winger Jimmy Johnstone, "Chopper" to match the, ahem, uncompromising style of renowned Chelsea defender Ron Harris, or Hibernian's own "Last Minute" Reilly, aptly putting into words the great striker Lawrie Reilly's ability to score vital late goals.

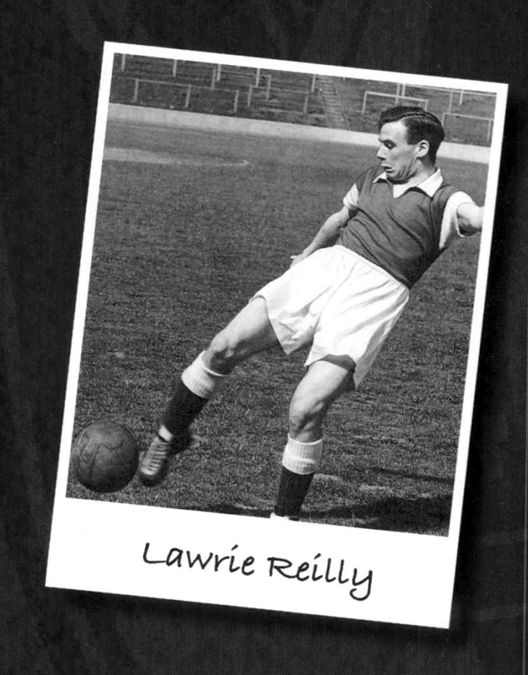

Lawrie Reilly

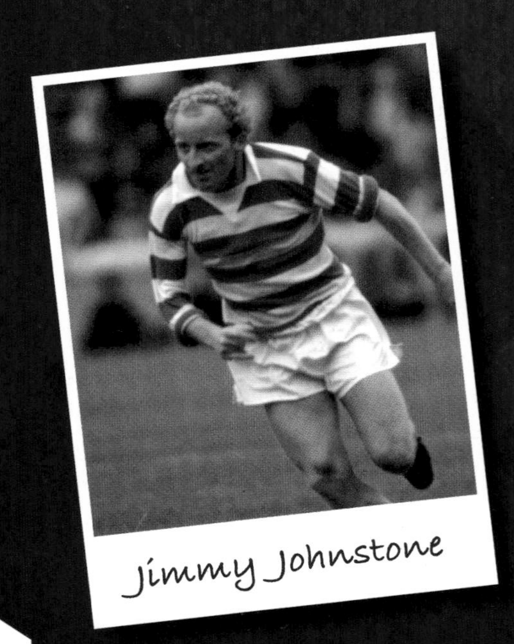

Jimmy Johnstone

Others may be more reflective of personality, or some personal characteristic, but all end up being an important part of the lasting appeal of players and help forge links between footballers and supporters.

Clubs too enjoy nicknames, just as the famous Hi-bees and city rivals Jam-Tarts do. Dundee United are "The Arabs", Ayr United "The Honest Men" and Motherwell "The Steelmen."

Other nations are just as keen on a good nickname, with some lingering long in the memory: "Psycho" Stuart Pearce renowned for his toughness, once trying to run off a broken leg; "Crazy Horse" Emlyn Hughes galloping upfield for Liverpool; Duncan "Disorderly" Ferguson, a fearsome Scottish striker who terrorised defences both sides of the Border, as well as any burglars foolish enough to break into his home; "Der Bomber" Gerd Muller, the German goal-scoring machine; Italian midfield maestro Andrea "Il Professore" Pirlo; or Eusebio, the Portugese superstar of the 60s and 70s known around the world as "The Black Pearl."

Even the greatest have nicknames, with Lionel Messi glorying in "La Pulga Atomica" – the atomic flea – perhaps reflecting his superpowers. And Edson Arantes do Nascimento is a mouthful that might leave many scratching their head – but you would certainly remember Brazil's all-time greatest, Pele.

Gerd Muller

Over the years, many stars who have graced the Easter Road turf have also had nicknames. So why not test your knowledge?

Which Hibernian players – past and present – match these nicknames: We've done the first one for you

Onion	Ally Brazil
Big Bob	Jim Herriot
The Quiet Man	John Burridge
Sodjer	John Hughes
Archie	Stuart Lovell
Le God	John Brownlie
The Squirrel	Franck Sauzee
Rocky	Alex Cropley
Budgie	John Blackley
Sloop	Ian Murray
Nid	Martin Boyle
Yogi	Ofir Marciano
Nicker	Scott Brown
Broonaldo	Barry Lavety
Basher	Pat Stanton
Benny	Bobby Johnstone

Answers on p.59

DANNY SWANSON

10 FACTS ABOUT OUR MIDFIELD MAESTRO

1 Danny was born in 1986. He suffered from a heart defect, which required several operations including a heart bypass when he was just 13.

2 He grew up in Leith, and was a childhood pal of central defender Darren McGregor.

3 Danny is 5ft 6in tall.

4 As a youngster, he played for Hutchison Vale and Leith Athletic.

5 His first professional club was Berwick Rangers, in 2005.

6 By the time he joined Hibernian in the summer of 2017, Danny had made almost 340 senior appearances.

7 He was a Scottish Cup winner with Dundee United in season 2009/10, and won the Johnstone's Paint Trophy with Peterborough in 2014 at Wembley.

8 Danny briefly played for arch-rivals Hearts, but has supported Hibs all of his life.

9 Danny scored 12 goals in 24 appearances last season for St Johnstone in the Premiership.

10 He is a great champion of mental health and well-being, having spoken about his own battles with depression.

NEW RECRUITS

#1
OFIR MARCIANO

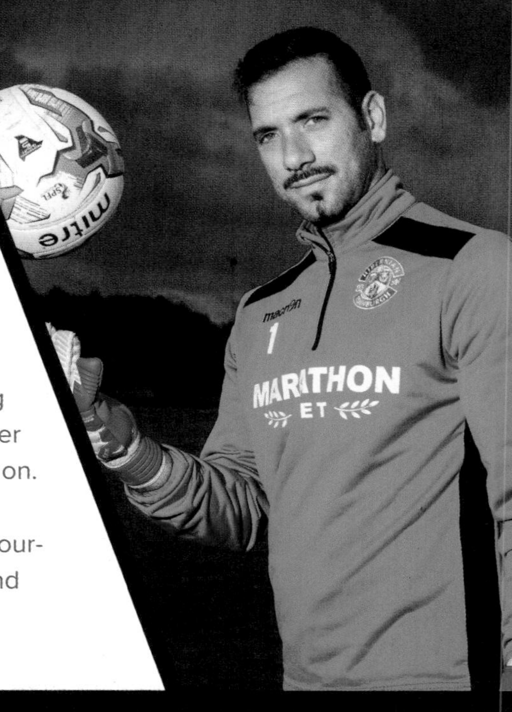

Clinching the long-term signature of Israeli international goalie Ofir Marciano after the big stopper's impressive loan spell at Hibernian was a key target.

Neil Lennon was delighted when the Club was able to secure "Rocky" on a lengthy deal over the summer, insisting that the Club had secured a top-class and developing keeper who would help create a strong defensive platform to build on.

The 6ft 4in Marciano signed from Israeli club Ashdod for a four-year term, and is delighted to have won his move to Scotland which has helped him regain his international place.

#8
VYKINTAS SLIVKA

Midfielder Slivka was signed from Italian Serie A giants Juventus in the summer on a three-year deal.

The 22-year-old midfielder has played around 20 times for his country, Lithuania, including appearing against Scotland at Hampden, adding to the growing stable of internationalists at Easter Road.

Standing well over 6ft tall, he signed for Juve in season 2012/13 and has played on loan in Italy's second tier and most recently with Den Bosch in the Netherlands.

Best employed in central midfield, Slivka is two-footed, composed, strong and mobile.

#9 DEIVYDAS MATULEVICIUS

Striker Deivydas Matulevičius signed from Belgian side Royal Mouscron in the summer.

A full Lithuanian international with more than 30 caps to his credit, the 6ft 3in centre-forward put pen to paper on a two-year deal.

An admirer of British football, he was delighted to join Hibernian: "I am very happy to now be a part of this club. It's a big step in my career and I will do everything I can to make it a successful season for us.

"I've always watched British football and the style of play will suit me - it's more physical and you need to have a lot of fight in every game. It's a big club with a big history and I'm really happy to be here."

#3 STEVEN WHITTAKER

The summer saw a homecoming for one of Hibernian's vaunted "golden generation" when 31-times capped Scotland international Steven Whittaker agreed a three-year deal.

The versatile defender and midfielder came through the Academy ranks at Easter Road alongside Kevin Thomson, Scott Brown, Derek Riordan and Gary O'Connor, and played in the youthful Hibernian team that excited Scottish football in the mid-2000s, culminating in the lifting of the League Cup in 2007.

Since leaving Hibernian, Steven has played for Rangers and for Norwich in both the top flight of English football and in the Championship.

WORDSEARCH QUIZ

Name ten Hibernian Managers or Head Coaches whose surnames are hidden in this puzzle:

T	H	J	M	S	T	A	N	T	O	N
L	R	S	N	I	L	L	O	C	X	L
Y	F	K	L	R	D	G	Z	N	L	R
D	E	X	C	K	L	L	K	U	B	H
N	N	L	R	N	K	E	B	X	M	W
O	L	S	K	M	T	N	N	I	P	N
M	O	B	P	C	R	R	L	N	T	L
R	N	B	N	U	A	L	W	T	O	Y
O	X	U	T	R	E	L	F	A	L	N
Y	N	T	B	R	Q	M	B	K	H	D
R	V	S	K	N	L	F	L	W	L	S

Answers on p.59

Hibernian Girls & Ladies continues to go from strength to strength – attracting more and more people to take part and with the women's first team re-establishing the Club at the top of the game.

Scottish Cup and League Cup wins over the past couple of seasons has seen Hibernian Ladies challenge the dominance of Glasgow City, and has also brought two UEFA Champions League outings for the team. In addition, three Hibernian players – Rachel McLauchlan, Joelle Murray and Kirsty Smith – were picked for the Euro 2017 Scotland squad.

All in all, the women's game continues to grow, and is now attracting more coverage in the media and on television, and in turn that has seen increased interest and sponsorship.

All of which made an appointment in the summer all the more necessary and all the more exciting.

Joelle Murray, the team's captain, was appointed by Hibernian Community Foundation – who run the Girls & Ladies – as Hibernian Girls Academy Manager.

She said: "This is an exciting time for the women's game and one I'm privileged to be part of.

"This role is one that I'm delighted to accept and look forward to the challenge during this era for the Girls and Ladies development. Opportunities for women to work full time within the game is limited, so to have this opportunity fills me with real excitement and gratitude to Hibernian Community Foundation for this investment."

Joelle has responsibility across the whole Academy including player development, technical development, recruitment, sports science and will also look to develop the Girls Performance Centre.

The club is also about encouraging participation, and in that regard help is always needed with volunteers essential to its success.

Charlie Bennet, Chief Executive of Hibernian Community Foundation, said:

"We are investing in the future of the women's game through Joelle's appointment, and she is exactly the right person at the right time to take things forward.

"But we also rely on the help of dedicated volunteers. While I would like to record our thanks for those who already commit valuable time and energy, we could do with more help as the club continues to grow!

"We need coaches, first-aiders and others. All coaches will have all their SFA coaching badges paid for by the club. This is an exciting opportunity to come in and work with a great bunch of girls within a very successful football club."

If you would like further information on Girls football at Hibernian please contact kmcewan@hiberniancommunityfoundation.org.uk.

WINNING TROPHIES

Scottish Division One (1890 – 1975); Scottish Premier Division (1975 – 1998); Scottish Premier League (1998 - 2013); Scottish Premiership (2013 – present)

Winners (4): 1903, 1948, 1951, 1952
Runners-up (6): 1897, 1947, 1950, 1953, 1974, 1975

Scottish Cup

Winners (3): 1887, 1902, 2016
Runners-up (11): 1896, 1914, 1923, 1924, 1947, 1958, 1972, 1979, 2001, 2012, 2013

Scottish League Cup

Winners (3): 1972, 1991, 2007
Runners-up (7): 1950, 1969, 1974, 1985, 1993, 2004, 2016

Division Two (before 1975); First Division (1975 – 2013); Scottish Championship (2013 – present)

Winners (6): 1894, 1895, 1933, 1981, 1999, 2017

Drybrough Cup

Winners (2): 1972, 1973

Summer Cup

Winners (2): 1941, 1964
(courtesy of Hibernian Historical Trust)

BEING 1ST

Hibernian were:

- involved in the first game conducted under floodlights.
- the first club in British top-flight football to have shirt sponsorship.
- the first club in Scotland to install under soil heating.
- the first club to have an electronic scoreboard.
- the first club to win successive First and Second Division Championships.
- the first club to produce a player to be capped by England whilst not playing in the English League - Joe Baker.
- the first club from Britain to play in Europe.
- the first British club to reach the European Cup semi-final.
- the first British club to beat Real Madrid.
- the first British team to score a European goal, scored by Eddie Turnbull.

QUIZ ANSWERS

Season Quiz (p16-17)

1. Kris Commons
2. Jason Cummings
3. Israeli
4. Efe Ambrose
5. Queen of the South
6. 8 – against Bonnyrigg Rose in the Scottish Cup at Tynecastle
7. Hearts
8. Aberdeen in the Scottish Cup semi
9. Brondby
10. Falkirk

Fontaine of Knowledge (p20)

1. True
2. False, sadly
3. True
4. No, False, it's goalies gloves for Rocky
5. True
6. True, he penned and performed a new Hibernian song
7. True, big-hearted Marv also launched an appeal post Grenfell Tower
8. False, thankfully
9. True, winning celebrations at Easter Road and Parkhead
10. True, born and bred a Leither

Spot the Ball (p43)

Ball D is the correct answer

What's in a nickname (p48-49)

Onion – John Brownlie; Big Bob – Jim Herriot; The Quiet Man – Pat Stanton; Sodjer – Alex Cropley; Archie – Stuart Lovell; Le God – Frank Sauzee; The Squirrel – Martin Boyle; Rocky – Ofir Marciano; Budgie – John Burridge; Sloop – John Blackley; Nid – Ian Murray; Yogi – John Hughes; Broonaldo – Scott Brown; Basher – Barry Lavety; Benny – Ally Brazil; Nicker – Bobby Johnstone

Wordsearch quiz (p54-55)

Stubbs; Turnbull; Stanton; Lennon; Fenlon; Miller; Collins; Shaw; Ormond; Blackley

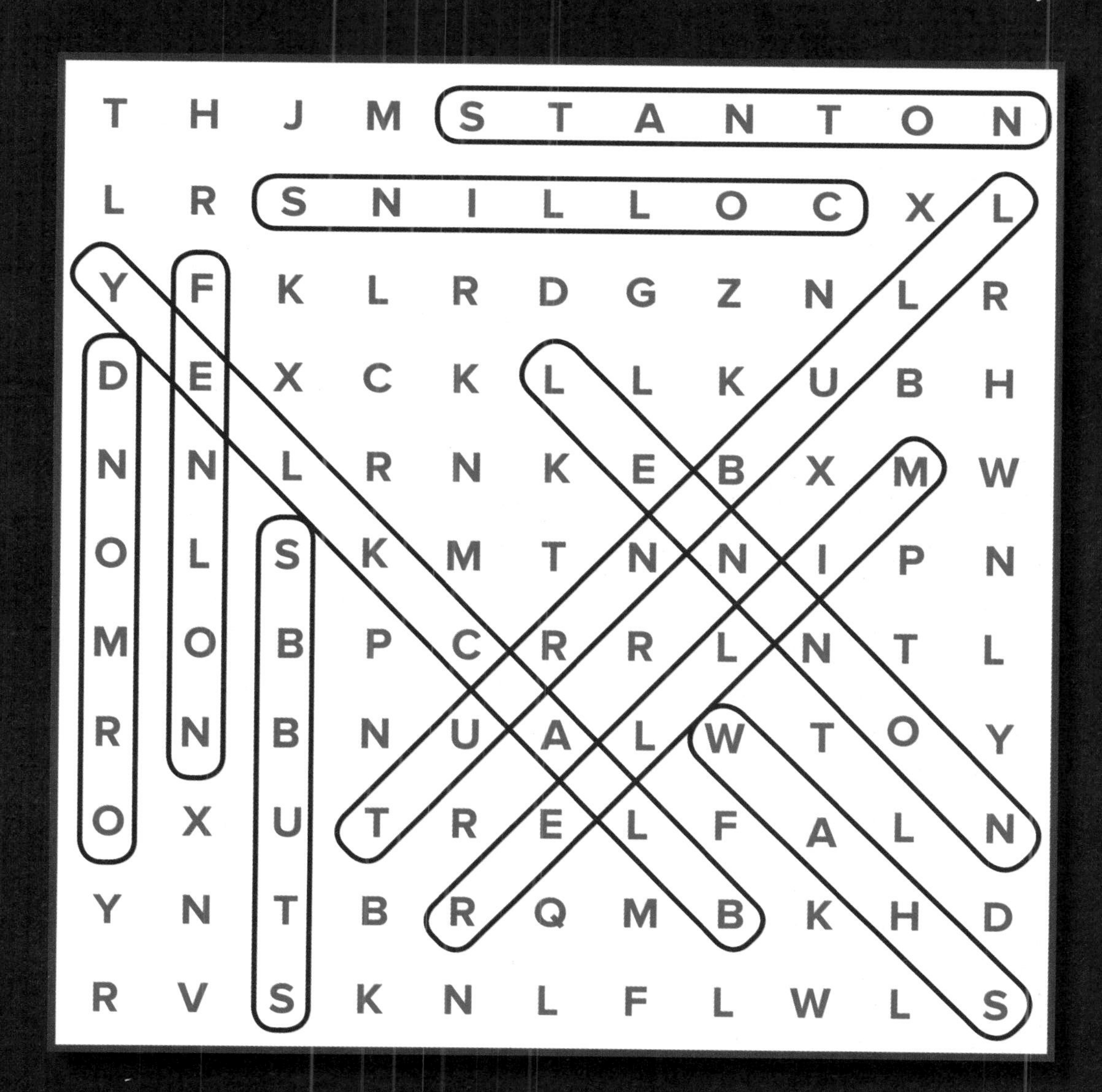

CLUB CONTACT INFORMATION

ADDRESS:
Easter Road Stadium, 12 Albion Place,
Edinburgh, EH7 5QG

EMAIL:
club@hibernianfc.co.uk
Tel: 0131 661 2159

TICKET OFFICE:
Ticket Office: tickets@hibernianfc.co.uk
Tel: 0844 844 1875

CONNECT WITH US ON SOCIAL MEDIA

TWITTER:
@HIBSOFFICIAL

FACEBOOK:
HIBERNIAN FOOTBALL CLUB OFFICIAL

INSTAGRAM:
HIBERNIANFOOTBALLCLUB

SNAPCHAT:
@HIBSOFFICIAL

CAN YOU FIND
Sunshine
The Leith Lynx
HIBERNIAN FC